TAKE TEN

TAKE TEN

THE ADULT TIMEOUT FOR WORK

Cynthia Chauvin
with Miles Chauvin

TAKE TEN

The Adult Timeout For Work

ISBN 13: 978-1-62154-983-3

Cover and Interior Design by Nu-ImageDesign.com

Image Copyright Billdayone, 2012

Used under license from Shutterstock.com

Author photography: Joe Henson

Bebas font courtesy: Ryoichi Tsunekawa

Published by:

Two Dragons International Inc.

Washington D.C. | New Orleans

www.twodragons.com

For special pricing on bulk sales contact

booksales@twodragons.com

For more information and companion audio products please visit

Cynthia's website:

www.cynthiachauvin.com

FOREWORD

My wife Cynthia has done thousands of psychic readings and hypnosis sessions for her clients. The insights in *Take Ten* come from these experiences.

This book and the other books in the *Take Ten* series along with *The 10 Ways*, and our audio CDs are all designed to empower you with the tools to change unproductive thoughts and behaviors.

Whether you use the products together, or separately, the information in each will help you have a better relationship with yourself and others.

Miles Chauvin

INTRODUCTION

Every behavior pattern you have created, started out with a base positive intent to protect you. The behavior may now be antiquated and no longer work to help you, but the intent still holds true.

The power to change these old behaviors lies in your ability to interrupt the patterns in your life and replace them with a broader perspective.

Take Ten was created to be a pattern interrupter, a simple yet effective way to take the moment before an unwanted behavior is repeated and instead fill that moment with insight.

These insights allow you to rethink your present course of action thereby opening you to more choices.

When you see new choices on how to experience a situation, you change your experience. Once an experience is changed, behavior is changed and thereby the outcome changes.

Changes are ecological. When you change one tiny part everything else starts to align itself with that new part. There is no such thing as a small change – it all has a big impact.

HOW TO USE THIS BOOK

The idea is of this book is to literally take ten. When you feel yourself drifting into a sea of depleting, derogatory or unsuccessful repetitive behavior take the book out and think to your self:

"What am I trying to see at this moment? How does this experience want to help me?"

Then flip to a page.

Drink the insight in and let it propagate and inform your thoughts about the situation you are dealing with.

"

Everybody pretends to be something-until they know who they are.

"

"

B elieve what you must; but you are what you will.

"

"

W e always have the answer.
We often forget the question.

"

"

Opinions need to be expanded or they become our dinosaurs -and eventually our extinction.

"

"

A nger is the last refuge to blame someone else for our outcome.

"

"

Wash your hands before you eat. Wash your thoughts before you speak.

"

"

L ife finds you when you are
ready for it.

"

"

When we speak clearly we see things clearly.

"

"

We have overvalued our experiences, and placed them as our God.

"

"

A ir: something you cannot see, but need to live. Spirit: just the same.

"

"

J udgment of one man eases the
conscience of many.

"

"

Take history and educate yourself from it, do not limit yourself with it.

"

"

We must dance to the music
that is playing.

"

"

If you are afraid to die, then you are afraid to live.

"

There are no choices until you decide there are choices.

"

L earning is not a process of studying what you have done, but seeing it with new eyes.

"

"

Wish for what you have; you already received it.

"

"

There is no victim without a perpetrator. BOTH exist because of one another, not in spite of one another.

"

"

There is meaning in everything. Whether that meaning is perceivable to us is another thing entirely.

"

"

Every time you are afraid of an ending, you are afraid of a beginning.

"

"

R epetition is not a penance but an opportunity.

"

"

We give ourselves a limited sense of who we are, and then we live up to it.

"

"

You aren't making a choice if you are afraid of a potential outcome. You are just reacting to a futurized event.

"

"

We create lack to grow faith. When we have faith we don't need to create the lack.

"

"

We fear that we will not get what we want; but we fear more that we will.

"

"

In war there are no victors, just survivors.

"

"

No fret, No regret.

"

"

When we are looking for self-justification from other people, we will do a job poorly or well. When we are self-justified, every job becomes a meditation and the end result perfect.

"

"

L ife is moving shit into manure, into fertilizer, then into a flower.

"

"

To meet our fate we must have Faith.

"

"

Jealousy, if allowed, rules our nature.

"

"

L ife is there to service you, not for you to service it.

"

"

The only thing that stands in the way of a dream becoming reality is a lack of Faith.

"

"

If I am angry, I am in fear and doubt about something I thought was safe.

"

"

Acceptance creates movement in anything that is stuck.

"

"

We don't create regret when we find purpose in our experience.

"

"

Watch and listen, and you will see.

"

"

Wherever there is a lie between two, there is a lie on both sides.

"

"

Anything you can think of is smaller than what you are worthy of.

"

"

L ife is always fair. We just don't
want to see what fair means.

"

"

There is no such thing as one man's guilt.

"

"

The most painful vision is to see oneself as other see you.

"

"

Trust in one's self is the ultimate foundation of good communication.

"

"

All forms of motivation are neither good nor bad just inspiration to move.

"

"

All people succeed who find the grand rhythm.

"

"

What is fear? A limitation not yet freed.

"

"

Other people effect our lives. We are the only one who can affect our lives.

"

"

First look. Then feel. Then see. Then speak. You'll keep your feet out of your mouth.

"

"

When we are worried about who we are supporting, it is because we are feeling unsupported.

"

"

T oday's problems are
tomorrow's wisdom.

"

"

The only thing that changes a perception is a larger canvas.

"

"

Expectation of failure creates.

"

"

L ive the moment and you dispel the illusion.

"

"

Quiet is the sound of God. Defense is the sound of the ego.

"

"

C an there be a beginning if there is no end?

"

"

To meet a friend and not an enemy is the nature of one who has survived and conquers their fears.

"

"

For every negative there is a positive, for every positive a negative. See both and we witness wholeness.

"

"

Crisis- The gift that pushes us beyond our fears and into change.

"

"

W hat we have is what we wished for.

"

"

The fact that Destiny and Freewill can, and do, co-exist is a Divine Paradox.

"

"

How you see the past defines your ability to have a future.

"

"

People don't want equality. They want to be superior to some, and inferior to others.

"

"

Our shekels are our shackles.

"

"

C hildren play games adults
have relationships.

"

"

A re they ignorant, or are you
arrogant?

"

"

Step out of the shadow of your own fear.

"

"

When you say you can't do something, you can't even attempt it; you're saying that God can't do it. Is that possible?

"

"

We are victims of the circumstances we create.

"

"

Everybody is the reluctant hero of his or her own life.

"

"

Money should enhance your life, not become your life.

"

"

Information is never loud or noisy; egos are.

"

"

L imitations are a part of the process.

"

"

When we are ready to move, mountains move. When we are not ready to move, molehills are mountains.

"

"

Perfectionism is a disease of low self-esteem.

"

"

R each for the stars. They are closer than you think.

"

"

R esistance is sometimes assistance.

"

"

T o watch people is to watch your self.

"

"

Opinions without judgment.

"

"

Whispering tales about other people is a loud commentary about your self.

"

"

L ittle fish in a pond, you don't know you are little until a big fish comes along.

"

"

R eactions are about the self and actions are about the other.

"

"

D on't be the problem you are trying to fix.

"

"

E ffectiveness is not measured
by outcome.

"

"

When there is gratitude there is no attitude.

"

"

If you didn't have the issue you wouldn't bring in the problem.

"

"

We don't call in failure we call in success and turn it into failure.

"

"

Judgments are jealousies in disguise.

"

"

You are the big channel of life turned down to the small channel of survival.

"

"

People let their creation create them rather than creating their creation.

"

"

Wherever we are stunted is where we don't get along with another.

"

"

When you can't find what you are looking for stop looking. You may have already found it.

"

"

The commonality between all
people is their differences.

"

There is no halfway Pathway.

"

When you blame yourself for your circumstances you can't change anything. But when you take responsibility for your circumstances you can change everything.

"

"

People who can't see potential in others can't see potential in themselves.

"

"

E motions are meant to create motion not reaction.

"

"

D o not act like other people think of you.

"

"

Abundance without wisdom is like a gun in the hands of a 2 year old.

"

"

All reality is constructed from imagination, thereby unreal.

"

"

Children do what they see until
they see what they do.

"

"

Where we fight to get out we never leave.

"

"

Opinions are like toilet paper: use once and throw away.

"

"

Being quiet is an action.

"

"

Some people make their title and some people are made by their title.

"

"

Judgment of another's choice is not necessary for us to make a choice.

"

"

It is childish to want other people to be adults.

"